The Floral Designer

The Floral Designer

USING COLOR AND TEXTURE
IN FLOWER ARRANGING

Joanna Sheen

Sterling Publishing Co., Inc.   New York

To Adrian and Pippa
for their help and patience!

Published in 1990 by
Sterling Publishing Co., Inc.
387 Park Avenue South
New York, New York 10016

First published in the U.K. in 1990 by Merehurst Press, London.
This edition published by arrangement with Merehurst Press. Available in
the United States, Canada and the Philippine Islands only.

Library of Congress Cataloging-in-Publication Data

Sheen. Joanna.
    The floral designer: using color and texture in flower arranging
/ Joanna Sheen.
        p. cm.
    ISBN 0-8069-7302-1
    1. Flower arrangement.   2. Dried flower arrangement.   3. Flowers Color.
        4. Wreaths.   5. Flower arrangement—Equipment and supplies.
I Title.
SB449.S465   1990
745.92—dc20   89-28281
                                                        CIP

Edited by Jane Struthers
Designed by Peartree Design Associates
Photography by Paul Grater
Styling by Joanna Sheen and Diana Hatherly
Typeset by Rowland Phototypesetting Limited, Bury St Edmunds, Suffolk
Color separation by Fotographics Limited, London–Hong Kong
Printed in Italy by New Interlitho S.p.A., Milan
Oasis is a registered trademark of
Smithers Oasis Company

PHOTOGRAPHIC CREDITS

The publishers would like to thank the following for the loan of their photographs:
Pp 8–9 reproduced by kind permission of the Netherlands Board of Tourism
Pp 10–11 reproduced by kind permission of the Netherlands Board of Tourism
Pp 14–15 © The National Trust Photographic Library/Neil Campbell Sharp, photographer
Pp 24–5 The National Trust Photographic Library/© Marin Dohrn
Pp 42–3 © The National Trust Photographic Library/Eric Crichton, photographer
Pp 58–9 © Hugh Palmer, photographer
Pp 74–5 © The National Trust Photographic Library/Eric Crichton, photographer
Pp 92–3 © The National Trust Photographic Library/Rob Matheson, photographer
Pp 108–9 © The National Trust Photographic Library/Neil Campbell Sharp, photographer
Pp 124–5 © The National Trust Photographic Library/Neil Campbell Sharp, photographer

CONTENTS

FOREWORD

If the flower arranger's world seems a sedate one, with little to disturb its calm image, Joanna Sheen's latest book is likely to come as a pleasant surprise. She makes it clear that new ideas are as vital to the successful practice of this decorative art as to any other, and, taking colour and texture as her theme, shows those areas where fresh ground can best be broken.

Grateful for the formal floristry training she received as a student, Joanna nonetheless believes that free-flowing and natural styles of flower arranging are more appropriate for the interiors of today, with less emphasis on rules, more on inspiration.

In the course of visiting many beautiful homes both large and small, I have long realised the value of flowers in any decoration scheme: however elegant a room, it needs their unique contribution. No one understands this better than Joanna and in reading her new book I have been fascinated by her skill and sensitivity in suiting an arrangement to its setting. She has used her own enchanting farmhouse home in Devon, and the homes of several friends, as background to most of the charming illustrations and there could be no better way of demonstrating her talents.

The assembly of each arrangement is discussed in detail but the book is designed to inspire rather than to instruct, and although its commonsense prose and splendid photography have an immediate appeal it is for the quality and originality of its ideas that it will be lastingly treasured.

Anne Lucey

ANNE LUCEY
Housing Editor, Ideal Home

WORKING WITH FLOWERS

*F*lowers have an immensely strong effect on us all. A bunch of flowers bought on impulse can cheer up a grey day, and a beautiful arrangement in a house can turn a dull room into a bright and cosy place. Bringing the garden inside is an old tradition that plays an increasingly important role in decorating our homes.

Although virtually any mix or combination of flowers looks quite lovely, whether in the wild or in the garden, their impact can be even stronger if they are carefully chosen for their colour as well as their shape and style.

Obviously, growing flowers in your garden (should you have one) is the cheapest way to obtain flowers for the house, but fresh flowers are so readily available nowadays that they are for sale at every possible outlet. Dried and silk flowers are easily bought from department stores and gift shops, as well as florists and other specialist outlets. The only flowers that I would never recommend displaying in your home are wild ones. These flowers should be enjoyed by us all when we visit the countryside, and that's where they look best. So leave them to flourish there and for the next visitor to enjoy!

This is one of the many vividly coloured stalls that can be seen and admired at a flower market in Amsterdam.

The flower industry has grown enormously over the last few decades, and now you can obtain many types of flowers all year round and from exciting countries overseas. Whether you wish to use native or imported flowers, it is good to be able to have that choice, and even if you have a flourishing garden (or window box!) it's fun to grow something a little bit different every now and then.

Flowers from many different countries have been used for the photographs in this book. Holland and Israel, both major flower-growing areas, are well represented, but I have also used kangaroo paw from Australia, gladioli from Brazil and native proteas from South Africa, as well as flowers from many areas of Great Britain and Europe.

When buying flowers, it is most important to ensure that they are very fresh, since flowers that are slightly past their best will only wilt and die on you a few hours after you've arranged them, which is both disappointing and frustrating. There are several points to remember when choosing flowers for a decoration. As well as the obvious considerations such as their colour and size, you should also decide whether you want something extra glamorous to give an exciting effect for one special evening, or whether you want something pretty but long-lasting to cheer up your home for a week or more. Scent may be another important factor to take into consideration. Whilst it can be wonderful to fill a whole sitting room or hallway with the perfume of flowers, the effect may not be so happy in a dining room, where a very strong perfume can put diners off their food.

There are many important hints and tips on keeping fresh flowers alive and perky for as long as possible, which I will elaborate on later (*see pp 16–17*). Despite that, some flowers simply last longer than others and therefore, no matter how hard you try, a sweet pea will always fade faster than a chrysanthemum! Enjoy each flower for its own delicacy and style, whether it's with you for a day or a week.

These serried ranks of tulips, forming marvellous sheets of colour, are just part of the massive bulb fields at Bollenveld de Zilk in Holland.

I am an ardent fan of both dried and silk flowers – they look so beautiful, and last and last no matter how high the central heating or how much you neglect them! The only attention they need is a quick dust every now and then.

As I am an extremely busy person, yet love to fill my home with loads of flowers, it suits me perfectly to spend quite a lot of thought and money on some silk and dried arrangements that I can then enjoy for weeks and months afterwards. In fact, I've had one particular arrangement for years! It can be a great deal of fun working with dried and silk flowers because you have so much time to get the arrangement just the way you want it. If you're not happy you can pull it all to pieces (carefully!) and rearrange it; the flowers will still be fine. On the other hand, if you mess around for too long with fresh flowers they will gradually wilt, and really prefer to be handled as little as possible. Having said that, one must also remember the special magic that only belongs to very beautiful fresh flowers, and nothing can beat the scent and sight of the first violets and lilies of the valley when they appear in my garden each year.

When you are choosing silk flowers,

don't be tempted to buy the cheapest you can find. It's often well worth spending a little more money and getting really top-quality silk flowers, since the colours and materials used are far superior to cheaper varieties. There are so many stunning silk flowers available nowadays, which is marvellous when one remembers the very first artificial flowers that were quite horrendous, garish and bore no resemblance to the real thing whatsoever. However, times have changed, thankfully, and the lovely soft colourings and vast range of types leaves the choice wide open. These days, the main problem I have is to choose which flowers to buy and which, reluctantly, to leave in the shop!

When dealing with silk and dried flowers, you will need very similar tools to those required for fresh flowers, but also a few extras, such as a very tough pair of wire cutters for the wired stems of silk flowers, and dry oasis in which to arrange them, rather than the normal wet type. The fact that these flowers need no water considerably increases the range of

This selection of flowers and foliage shows just how versatile, realistic and durable silk flowers can be.

containers that you can use, and something that would either be damaged by water or is porous can come into its own at long last.

Dried flowers have become extremely popular over the past few years, and are far more widely available than they were. There is still nothing to beat the satisfaction of drying your own flowers from your own garden, and taking time and trouble, using silica gel and other labour-intensive methods, to produce your own little treasures. Even so, many of us are far too busy to actually dry the flowers ourselves and would prefer to devote our spare time to arranging flowers that have already been dried. If this holds true for you, you'll find that there are innumerable varieties available from specialist dried flower shops, department stores or smaller gift shops. Have a good prowl around and you'll be amazed at the choice that is available to you.

Flowers that have been dried can be divided into two categories – the ones that have retained their natural colouring and those that have been given a little help with some dye. Although the natural ones may have more appeal initially, don't reject out of hand the flowers and leaves that have been lightly dyed as they can be extremely effective when mixed with other suitable colours, and of course they do make the arrangement look more bright and colourful than it would otherwise have been.

The only other contrast I would make between silk, fresh and dried flowers is that silk flowers are so wonderfully clean to work with! All you have to clear up are a few trimmed ends of wired stalks. When I was preparing the arrangements of fresh flowers in this book I managed to get water, green stalks, petals and bits everywhere, and succeeded in creating an equal amount of mess when I did the dried flower arrangements. I have no idea where all that mess comes from, but come it does. So, if you want to halve the work of clearing up, spread an old sheet over the area on which you will be working, and then you'll be able to gather up all the bits at once. The lack of mess created when working with silk flowers is hardly a major consideration, but it is certainly an extra bonus!

The variety of textures, colours, shapes and sizes of dried flowers and grasses makes them ideal for many arrangements.

If you are a very keen flower arranger, then I suppose that the ideal is to have a good-sized piece of garden that you can devote to growing flowers for cutting and some for drying and preserving. Unfortunately, this is a luxury that is denied to many of us, and therefore one has to find other alternatives. However, if you are lucky enough to have such an area to spare in your garden, you can have great fun planning how best to fill it. I would always choose to grow plants and flowers that are never available commercially, or only at a price.

Think about the colour schemes that you choose time and time again for your arrangements, and then plan to grow flowers and plants in your chosen colours. My particular favourite is white, and I would happily have white, or white and silver arrangements all over the house, all year round. If you are very keen on silver, grey or variegated foliage, then concentrate on growing those; they never seem to be easily available from commercial florists.

There are many unusual colourings available, and you'll get a good idea of the wide selection by reading through a few seed catalogues. Even if you have only a few of these unusual items, they can be the stars of your arrangements and cost very little if produced from your own garden. Shapes that are out of the ordinary can also be most useful in an arrangement and these structural plants can be easily grown in the garden but often prove impossible to track down in florists' shops.

You can grow plants that offer large attractive leaves, such as those that belong to the bergenia family, hostas or large grasses. Another plant that is very popular with me is astrantia; I grow it in both pink and white varieties.

Another bonus of raising your own flowers for arranging, especially if you confine yourself to particular colour schemes, is that they will look wonderful while they grow. One-colour gardens are frequently stunning, though you might find that your own version looks so beautiful that you can't bear to cut any of the flowers!

A colourful view of the herbaceous border at Mompesson House, Wiltshire.

Once you have picked or bought the flowers and got them home, the first and most important step is to condition them. Never think that because they are freshly picked from the garden, or have just been delivered to your florist, that they are ready to be arranged. If you ignore this conditioning stage you do so at your peril, as the arrangement will droop in hours and you'll lose so much of the enjoyment you could have gained from the flowers. This rule also applies to foliage.

The basic requirement of flowers and foliage is a good long drink of water, but first you must make it as easy as possible for the plant material to take up the water. For woody or thick stems, therefore, you should smash the ends with a hammer, and make an angled cut across any other stems, preferably under water to reduce the risk of trapping any air bubbles that will prevent the water being taken up the stems. You should also strip off any foliage or flowers that will be under water, as they will simply rot and not only smell but also speed up the natural ageing process of the plant material.

There are many differing views on which treatment suits which flowers. I have tried every tip that I have ever read or had passed on to me by friends, and have found that ideas like mixing in an aspirin or adding gin to the water (better to add it to the flower arranger, in my opinion!) all have a slight effect but are not one hundred per cent successful. I have found the best solution is as follows:

> Mix together 300ml (½ pint) of water with 300ml (½ pint) of clear lemonade and 5ml (1 tsp) sugar. The flowers seem to last better in this than any other mixture.

Flowers are happiest when in a nice cool room, and if they are in one that is very warm the blooms will not last as long as they should. However, if there is a cooler room available that you could move the flowers to at night, you may prolong the life of the arrangement. Keep topping it up with water and change it frequently – so many people forget how thirsty flowers are, and when they are in oasis it is especially important to keep replenishing the water; check it at least once a day.

These flowers are having a long drink of water before they are arranged.

Bearing in mind all the different types of flower arrangements that one can create, from elaborate fresh displays to miniature dried ones, the list of containers that can be useful is enormous. As a keen flower arranger it is very easy to get carried away when one sees a lovely vase, whether it's a new one in a shop or a beautiful antique one in a sale or junk shop. My advice is that if you really want it, and it is affordable, then you should buy it when you see it. I'm still haunted by containers that I've seen in little antique shops and have thought I would go back and buy later, only to find that they've always been sold. Very annoying!

There are two possible approaches to containers: either you can collect and hoard them as I do or you can go out, having planned a particular arrangement and its position in your house, and buy a container especially for the purpose. In the case of a dried or silk arrangement it could well be in use for many a month, and so it is important that the container is exactly what you want.

The variety of materials is amazing—and is of no help to anyone indecisive as there is no doubt that one is spoilt for choice! A large contributory factor has to be the intended position of the arrangement and the style and furnishings of the room. You must also consider the style of the arrangement.

Glass is always one of my favourites as there are so many wonderful colours from which to choose. Using marbles in a clear glass container is one of the best new ideas in flower arranging to have emerged in years; by using a plain clear vase and then having a selection of different coloured marbles, one can ring the changes from a brilliant blue arrangement to a soft pink or burgundy one merely by altering the colour of the marbles used in the vase. Another favourite of mine, which I was shown at the Constance Spry Flower School, is to use the glass from smashed windscreens (windshields) as a covering for the mechanics of a modern arrangement. I have acquired a large box of glass shavings and general rubbish from my friend's glassware studio, and you can see the effect on page 51.

These baskets and pots make ideal yet unusual containers for arrangements.

Baskets are always popular with flower arrangers because they blend so well with the flowers. It pays to hunt around for some unusual baskets as they add so much more to a display. On pages 122–3 you will see an attractive dried arrangement in a basket made with lavender stalks entwined around the edge, and you can also find pastel-coloured baskets decorated with beautiful stencil work; such baskets are definitely available if you look for them.

Wooden containers always work well with flowers, probably because the wood, being a natural substance, blends well with the plant material. Boxes are one of the most effective containers of all, and over the years I've collected all shapes and sizes, both in rough and smooth wood.

There are two other main categories of container: china or pottery, and metal. When you are thinking of a more classic or formal arrangement, there is nothing to beat a really beautiful traditional silver rose bowl, or a special porcelain dish. Again, one can collect these containers over a long time, and with luck, you may own some silver or pewter vases that have been handed down through the family. I have a particular enthusiasm for pewter as I feel it goes so well with flowers, without being as formal as silver. Copper is another good metal to mix with flowers, and I always jump at any opportunity to acquire a copper jug or container when I find a good-quality one lurking in an antique shop. In some cases, metal containers may leak because of poorly soldered or welded joints, in which case I put them into my dried and silk repertoire. Alternatively, you can line them with another, watertight, container if you really want to use them for fresh flowers.

Ceramic containers can be very inexpensive and versatile. Cream and grey containers are often just as useful as white ones, as they can blend into the background more easily.

Always keep an open mind on what might be useful as a container, because often something unusual, from a tea cup and saucer to a soup tureen, can turn a pretty arrangement into a real conversation piece.

A selection of some of the china and glass containers that can be used for flowers.

At some time or other, nearly all of us have wanted, or needed, to create an arrangement yet been at a loss to find enough flowers and foliage. Perhaps it's at one of those times of the year when there is little in the shops (and what there is at a high price) and even less in the garden. Well, don't despair, for a quick hunt through your fridge or larder could reveal all sorts of treasures that are ideal for an arrangement.

In the photograph above you can see a selection of fruit and vegetables that would all look interesting and eye-catching in an arrangement. There are some very unusually-coloured vegetables, and their shapes can add an element of excitement to a collection of flowers. Globe artichokes and aubergines (eggplants) are just two vegetables that create an impact when used like this. On pages 138 and 139 you will see an arrangement of fruits and vegetables that contains no flowers at all, yet is still very attractive.

Accessories are also an important factor when creating an arrangement, and sometimes placing a small figurine or ornament near the display can greatly add to its impact. Other ideas, such as bows with dried flowers, and marbles with modern displays, can look wonderful, and you can see similar ideas such as the one shown on page 46, where some lilies were placed near a treasured photograph as a tribute. Never be afraid to try new ideas and possibilities, as there are countless combinations of flowers, containers and surroundings. I hope you have fun while you discover some of them!

Facing page: *Coloured glass marbles create extra interest in arrangements.* Above: *Fruits and vegetables can complement flowers.*

PEACHES AND CREAM

A walk through crunchy leaves
that are turning into
glorious shades of red and
gold – there's nothing like it for lifting
one's spirits. I think that's partly due
to the fabulous shades of the leaves.
All the colours of autumn, or fall,
are warm, cheerful tones, and they
help lift depression and cheer one up.

There are many images that these
colours bring to mind, from the
flames in a real log fire to thoughts
of warmer weather and peaches and
cream. Many subtle blends of these
colourings work well together and they
can be amongst the prettiest of flower
arrangements.

The range of flowers, both fresh
and otherwise, that are available in
these peachy tones is perhaps not
quite as large as that of other
shades, such as pink or yellow, but
nevertheless there are plenty from
which to choose. A vase containing
nothing but leaves, in various shades
of red, gold and green, would look
wonderful, the only drawback being
the speed with which they sometimes
drop. Glycerined leaves are also
very pretty, especially beech leaves,
which turn a marvellous coppery
colour. Berries, leaves and other
seasonal offerings can make a
splendid collection in a casual
setting.

*Red maples, with their beautiful leaves, are
a spectacular sight in the autumn.*

The beauty and subtlety of this mosaic surface (*see facing page*) could easily be overpowered by the strong colours of some flowers, but these tones of peach and green act as the perfect foil. I used a mixture of peach roses, white stephanotis and small white Michaelmas daisies, with small pieces of variegated foliage picked from my garden.

This is a three-quarter facing arrangement, with the sides continued round to the back, and I taped some wet oasis to the beige ceramic container—a simple flat dish on a small stem. The leaves were positioned first, ensuring a good mixture of varieties. I then arranged the roses, evenly spacing them so that they looked balanced when viewed from any angle, and then filled in with the stephanotis and daisies. The overall effect is very soft and pretty, with deeper patches of colour created by the roses.

My dried flower arrangement (*see below*) has a very different mood, and is much more cheeky. The container is an old tobacco jar minus its lid, and I wouldn't normally put flowers in it as their water would ruin the wood. However, in this instance the dry oasis used to hold dried flowers presents no problems. The mix of dried flowers includes many pink, amber, yellow and cream tones of statice, and some brown and green poppy seed heads, all of which complement the pine dresser and the objects on it.

I trimmed the dry oasis to fit inside the tobacco jar, then created a basic shape with the statice by placing a tall flower in the centre and working in circles down towards the bottom of the arrangement. Then I added the poppy seed heads to give a contrast. This little pot can now sit happily on my dresser all through the winter, providing some permanent colour.

The textured backgrounds enhance both these arrangements, giving them an extra dimension and enhancing the colours.

These 'Enchantment' lilies (*see facing page*) are great favourites of mine, but do watch out for their pollen, which stains very easily. The best remedy is to break off the stamens before you start to arrange them, and then no damage will be done. The red, orange and yellow colours of these lilies give an overall blend of warm, autumnal colours, which are really enhanced by the coppery marbles in the vase. To create a similar effect, fill about two-thirds of a clear glass vase with marbles – don't add any more or it will be difficult to arrange the flowers. Then top up the vase with water and you'll be able to see the marbles gleaming and shining. Having prepared your base, you can now add the flowers.

Making a garland (*see below*) isn't as simple as arranging the lilies, but the trick is to work slowly and methodically—garlands aren't nearly as complicated as they look. This one is a collection of pale peach dried flowers with leaves and grasses, and is assembled by making up small bunches of the plant material and wiring them together. Having wired the first bunch, wire the second bunch to the stems of the first, repeating this with more bunches until you are happy with the length of your garland. The ribbon bows can be attached later with wire. It is also useful to wire pieces of ribbon or cord to either end, so that the garland can be tied in its chosen position.

Garlands make wonderful decorations at any time of year, and can be created just as successfully with dried, silk or fresh flowers, or even just with such foliage as holly and ivy at Christmas time. When using peaches and cream colourings, it is easy to choose tones which will blend together successfully; just select flowers that are very similar to the main colour, with a blushing cream as the lightest shade, and a deeper peach as the darkest. The fact that fewer flowers seem to grow in natural peachy tones makes this all the more special as a colour scheme, and is popular with brides.

Below: *The soft peachy tones of this garland blend well with the tree.* Facing page: *This vase of lilies would brighten up any room.*

I t is important to consider style as well as colour when you are planning an arrangement. I wanted to make a display to complement my treasured tapestry, and so I knew that the shape and style would have to be as traditional as the backing, yet still maintain a distinct identity of its own.

Because I wanted this to be a permanent arrangement I chose dried flowers and foliage, beginning with some glycerined eucalyptus leaves which are a marvellous warm cream. To do this, choose some attractive and fresh branches with perfect leaves, and crush the bottom 5cm (2in) of stem with a hammer. Then place the branch in a container of equal amounts of glycerine and boiling water and allow to soak for between one and six weeks until the leaves have turned to your desired colour. Keep topping up the solution as it must not dry out. To blend with them, I found some small peachy-pink roses and some carnations with the most wonderful dusky rose tones. When considering the best type of container, I decided that the pink-peach theme would be best supported by a small copper trough which I discovered on one of my tours of junk shops. Its main trouble is that the seams in the copper are very poor and it doesn't hold water very well, so it suits dried flowers better than fresh, although I have used it for both and always line the container with polythene before filling it with water.

Basically this is a traditional triangular facing display, and I began it with the highest central point and then added the two extremities to make the basic shape so that I could decide how large to make the arrangement. Once I had completed the bare bones I was able to fill in with the dried flowers—a process that takes some time as there are so many of them and I like them to be tightly packed together. As a finishing touch I added a few grasses, which gave a softening effect to the display.

The subtle tones of the dried flowers and foliage used in this arrangement bring out the beautiful colours of the background tapestry. When making an arrangement to complement and enhance an existing feature in a room it is very important that the two should live together in harmony and not vie for attention or clash with each other.

Both these arrangements are very casual and don't involve any mechanics, looking as though a bunch of flowers has been placed in the container with no arranging at all. Don't you believe it! Just because I said there were no arranging mechanics doesn't mean it didn't take me quite some time to carefully position the height and weight of each flower until the arrangements were nicely balanced!

The dried flowers in the jug (*see below*) were planned to blend with the terracotta velvet curtains in my hallway. It is so dark there that fresh flowers never seem bright enough to show up well, and pot plants never last because there isn't enough light for them, but dried flowers are perfectly happy and these warm tones now make my hall look very cosy and welcoming indeed. The dried flowers include everlasting flowers (helichrysum), statice and amaranthus in various shades of rust, gold and yellow, with some green amaranthus to soften the effect. When strong colours are used in an undiluted display they can be a little overpowering,

The marvellous textures of dried flowers are seen to their full advantage and splendour when viewed against the backdrop of this velvet curtain.

so it's often a good idea to introduce a gentle colour, such as green, grey or cream, into the arrangement to soften it slightly. Here, I placed one variety of flowers into the jug at a time to ensure there was an even spread of colour.

In the collection on the dressing table (*see below*), there is a lovely mix of garden flowers and commercially-grown blooms; I like to see strong florists' flowers blended with softer, gentler garden varieties. Having found some peach carnations as a base, I added some gorgeous cream stocks and astrantia flowers from the garden. Since this arrangement was intended for a bedroom, I thought it would be nice to add some scent with a few large cream freesias, which always smell so strongly. The result is an unstructured bouquet of pastel flowers that give out a fabulous scent and make the dressing table look very feminine. The ceramic vase is a standard shape that I use very frequently because it lends itself to any quick arrangement of flowers and doesn't demand a well thought out and complicated display as some containers do.

This simple mixture of scented florists' and garden flowers in pastel colours makes a pretty decoration for a dressing table without being too overpowering.

Peaches and cream is an extremely popular colour scheme for weddings, and provides plenty of scope in the choice of flowers whatever the season.

The wedding buffet (*see previous page*) shows how well the peaches and cream theme lends itself to wedding flowers. The dainty flowers on top of the cake make it look quite lovely and link it to the table arrangement. I mixed the coppery-peach roses with some paler pinky-peach roses to give an overall softness to the arrangement, and added some creamy orchids and coppery-orange crocosmia for extra definition and texture, plus a few creamy freesias for their scent and colour. I made the table arrangement from two long, extended triangular facing arrangements and placed them back to back; as it was intended for a buffet table, it would be seen from all angles and so the flowers had to look as good when viewed from the back as from the front.

When I was planning a table centre for a less formal occasion last summer I decided that an edible centrepiece might be an idea, hence this arrangement of nasturtiums (*see below*). There are many edible flowers, and it's great fun to experiment with them; for example, you could scatter pansies, borage or rose petals over a salad. However, do check first that you haven't chosen anything poisonous, and do wash off any aphids that may be lurking among the petals! The peppery flavour of nasturtiums is delicious in salads, and their bright oranges and reds look marvellous against green salad leaves.

The soft colours of old wood (*see facing page*) in our lovely local tea rooms blend very well with this romantic arrangement of peach and ivory roses, with gold kangaroo paw flowers chosen for their unusual shape. The overall design is traditional with a twist! The container is a flat black ceramic dish with wet oasis taped into it, and the arrangement was then built up from the centre outwards. The water should always be kept topped up, as the flowers will drink more water than you might imagine.

Below: *Nasturtiums turn a green salad into something special.* Facing page: *The wooden shutters blend well with these flowers.*

Looking at this arrangement makes me realise how very much I like silk flowers. It was great fun to create and I'll be able to enjoy the finished basket of flowers for many years to come.

I chose a honey-coloured basket to tone with the warm hues of the flowers, with some green leaves, such as beech, to add a contrasting colour, and found a variety of flowers to provide different textures. For the main blooms I chose creamy peonies and pinky-peach full-blown roses, with some dark orange-peach freesias and crocosmia to contrast with their fullness and roundness.

To make the arrangement, first I filled the basket with blocks of dry oasis, taping them securely but discreetly to the sides. I then began by placing the leaves in position and added the large focal points – the roses and peonies—before filling in with the daintier flowers.

This colour scheme of flame blends very well with many textiles and other surfaces such as wood or stone. I particularly like using this colour combination with dark woods, such as rosewood or mahogany, since they complement the warm tones in the flowers much better than lighter woods like pine, light oak or elm.

As I've already said, silk flowers are wonderfully versatile and they can be of such high quality that it is hard to distinguish them from the real thing. If they are to be a fairly permanent arrangement it is a good idea to dust them regularly, as too much accumulated grime could spoil them. One very effective (and easy) way to dust them is with a hair dryer on a low setting—you can then blow the dust off them in a few seconds.

I suppose the only drawback with silk flowers is that they have no scent, but even that can be remedied. You can buy a bottle of the perfumed oil that matches one of the flowers – such as rose oil for silk roses—and place it in or near the flowers so that it gently releases its fragrance and adds to your enjoyment of the flowers.

A basket of silk flowers, such as this one, makes an ideal present for someone – if you are well acquainted with the decorative scheme of their house, or know of their favourite colours. As they need virtually no maintenance at all, silk flowers are perfect for people who lead very busy lives.

Sometimes I think that photographs displayed by themselves, no matter how cherished, can look rather lost, yet the trick is to find an ornament or floral decoration that complements the photograph rather than detracts from it. I decided to use the frame of the photograph (*see below*) as the inspiration for my arrangement, letting the pinks, yellows and sage greens dictate my choice of flowers. I felt dried flowers would be best, and chose a collection including yellow roses, heather and statice. Heather can be a pretty yet delicate addition to any arrangement, whether dried or fresh, and there are so many colours and types of heather that you should be able to find something to arrange all year round, especially if you grow some yourself.

The deep green furnishings of this room and dark wood of the table (*see facing page*) are the perfect foils for orange or peach colour schemes, so here I made an informal arrangement of soft peach carnations and bright orange crocosmia in a copper jug. The contrast between the two shapes of flower is interesting, with the gentle contours of the carnations and the sharp points of the crocosmia. When working with jugs of this shape, it is not easy to use any formal mechanics and in fact, just placing the flowers in the jug gives a much more relaxed feel. The height of the arrangement must be decided first and then you must take care to cover as many stems as possible as they can look ugly when visible either at the front of the arrangement or within it.

All these orange, flame and peach colours can be very beautiful if used carefully and with gentle colours to accompany them. Orange often looks very harsh if it is mixed with another hard colour and the result can be striking but not so pretty, restful or attractive. Soft shades such as cream and grey blend so well with the copper colours found in flowers and foliage that the overall display may contain several components that are hard and bright in colouring, but nevertheless look very pleasing when separated by softer colours.

These two arrangements show the effectiveness and impact gained when flowers are chosen to complement their surroundings.

WHITER SHADES OF PALE

*W*hite is one of the most
beautiful colours in
nature, in my opinion.
*Many people might disagree, instead
loving the bright vivid shades of
summer, while others opt for the
oranges and flames of the previous
chapter. However, when one is
thinking of flowers as a room
decoration, it is easy to fit white
ones into almost any colour scheme
or interior design. I also feel that
white flowers have a glowing, almost
luminous, appearance that looks very
clean and fresh. One of the greatest
plus-points of white flowers is that you
can mix lots of them together and
they will all look lovely.
Nevertheless, there is one important
rule to remember: you can't mix very
large impressive flowers with those
that are small and dainty, as you
lose the charm of the tiny flowers and
diminish the majesty of the larger
ones.*

   *Keeping to a completely white
colour scheme has become quite
popular in gardens today, and it can
look just as effective in the house. One
often thinks of wedding flowers as
being white, but there are many more
casual white flowers that can be
arranged in a very pretty way without
seeming too formal.*

*One of the most famous single-colour
gardens of the 20th century – the White
Garden at Sissinghurst, Kent.*

All the flowers in this fireplace display are silk, which means that once you have arranged them they can stay in place (with the odd bit of dusting every now and then) for months or even years, and still look lovely. Obviously, any arrangement of this size is not cheap, whether it is composed of flowers that are dried, fresh or silk, but at least it will give a great deal of pleasure once it is completed.

The container is a classic white ceramic bowl-shaped vase that is very useful for fruit, flowers or as an ornament in itself. Here, I filled the container with dry oasis, holding it firmly in place with white oasis tape. Fixing the oasis in position is even more important than usual with such a large arrangement as this, as it is very heavy and can easily slip. Nothing is more infuriating than spending ages arranging the flowers only to watch them gently slide

over, whether backwards or forwards! Having secured the oasis, I then started work on the outer points of the arrangement, using lupins, wisteria and rhododendrons to establish the height and width, then created a fan shape around the outside. I then filled in with the large flowers: the peonies, chrysanthemums and the full roses which I placed in the centre. Next, I added the artificial plums and greengages as a feature, and spread

These white silk flowers fill my enormous fireplace. Although not cheap to make, such an arrangement is an investment as it will look good for many months to come.

them evenly through the flowers. Finally, I filled in any gaps with irises.

The overall result is one of light, bright splendour, and this type of arrangement can be placed at floor level, on a grand buffet table or even on a pedestal.

The white longiflorum lilies (*see below*), are one of my very favourite flowers. To me, they have a beauty and classical elegance that outshines many other flowers, and in the arrangement here I have given them a period feel, as I think they are highly evocative. They look lovely on their own in a simple design like this, but they can also be very effective in a mixed pedestal display. Very often they are used in solemn arrangements, but they make marvellous celebratory wedding flowers too. I didn't use any mechanics for this arrangement; just filled the simple silver vase with water (which must be topped up frequently as lilies are very thirsty) and placed each flower in turn to give different levels and angles for extra interest and form. Sometimes it is the simple arrangements that are the best.

The two white arrangements (*see facing page*) are a very effective way of brightening up a staircase or hallway for a festive occasion. To make each one, I attached a small dome of wet oasis, encased in its own plastic container (these domes, which are easily bought ready-assembled, can also be used to make pew ends) on to the banisters. I then covered all the visible oasis with flowers and foliage as though I were making a perpendicular table arrangement, placing all the outer flowers first to get a good size and shape, and then worked out from the centre. The foliage is a mixture of variegated garden shrubs, including pittosporum and *Alchemilla mollis* flowers, and for the white flowers I chose roses, carnations and freesias.

White flowers have many moods. The longiflorum lilies (below) are very elegant whilst the large posies of flowers (facing page) are more informal.

This is a lovely relaxed collection of all my favourite white spring flowers: lilac, irises, tulips and longiflorum lilies. I'm particularly fond of using white lilac in arrangements because it is dependable and lasts very well, making it excellent value. The other flowers also last fairly well and, if they have plenty of water, will give many days of pleasure. For the container I chose a formal ceramic vase with no handles that looks most effective with a fan-shaped arrangement.

One normally associates tulips and irises with bright colours: perhaps yellow and red for tulips and blue and yellow for irises. Nevertheless, I think they look wonderful in this white collection and the overall effect is one that I could look at for ages. Flowers can be a very relaxing sight if their colours are soft and harmonious, and the shapes soft and pleasing, but if you choose such bright colours as red and orange, the effect can be quite the reverse, lifting and cheering you up whenever you feel miserable.

The different scents and shapes of this arrangement give it plenty of interest, yet the shades of white ensure that it is relaxing and easy to live with.

This arrangement of 'Paper White' narcissi and gypsophila can fill a room with its scent, and it will spread throughout the house if placed in an open space. It is the narcissi, of course, that have such a lovely and overwhelming smell, and they are also very pretty to look at. The ivory container blends well with the flowers, which I held in place with special oasis intended for spring flowers such as narcissi, daffodils, tulips, hyacinths and so on. If you try to use ordinary wet oasis you will find that stalks merely split or bend, making your task virtually impossible, so it is well worth buying a block of the correct oasis. Alternatively you can use marbles or wire netting. I arranged the narcissi flowers and leaves in a rounded shape, then added lots of very small pieces of gypsophila so that the overall shape would be easier to control.

The white irises (*see facing page*) are a good example of how just a few flowers can be as effective as bunches and bunches of them. This arrangement uses a pin-holder set in a low tray, on to which the irises are placed. Position the tallest flower first, then work down towards the base. Fill the tray with lumps of broken glass to hide the pin-holder (you can use the glass from a broken windscreen [windshield]), then top up with water. As irises are water-loving plants, I feel that this arrangement works very well.

*Whether a mixture of flowers are used (*below*) or just one variety (*facing page*), white flowers can look very dramatic.*

Although I work with dried flowers quite frequently, it is not often that I use only white ones. Somehow, white is not a colour that one associates with dried flowers, perhaps because so many flowers tend to turn cream or beige when they are dried. Admittedly, these are creamy-white, but the overall effect is charming. Being entirely made up of shades of white and cream, this arrangement would fit into almost any colour scheme and is a very peaceful and restful collection.

The basket is particularly attractive, with twigs and moss woven into its base. I secured some dried flower oasis into the

base of the basket with a little glue, then arranged a fairly dense covering of statice, or sea lavender. To fill this out, I added white daisies and edelweiss, cream statice and cow parsley.

Baskets lend themselves very well to dried arrangements and are useful containers; not only can they be quickly

The many tiny heads of dried flowers make this basket an endless pleasure to look at.

lifted up for dusting, but they are also quite sturdy and are not easily knocked off tables – a necessary consideration in many homes where pets and children are among the occupants!

M any flowers that are officially
described as white really contain
tinges of other colours too,
making them yellowy-white, as in the
photograph shown here, pinky-white or
even bluish-white. When working with
such flowers, I find it most successful to
use only pure white flowers together,
just creamy-yellow or all flowers with a
pink blush. Otherwise, the very mixture of
shades and tints can distract the eye and
detract from the overall success and
impact of the arrangement. In fact, if you
look closely at some of the flowers you
believe to be pure white, you may well be
surprised at how many of them do not
come into that category at all, but are,
in fact, flecked or tinged with other colours.

For this arrangement I used
yellowy-white flowers, choosing a mixture
of spider chrysanthemums, white gladioli,
spray daisies and white pinks. The
variegated foliage was chosen for its pale
green colouring, which accentuates the
yellowy shades of the flowers. To make
the arrangement, I taped a block of wet
oasis into the bottom of a classic-shaped
ceramic vase, then made a standard
triangular facing display, building up the
height and width first, filling in with some
of the larger flowers and finally adding
some small flowers. To enhance the
formal and elegant feel of the arrangement,
I used a container with a pedestal base.
This gave extra height and importance to
the display. Nevertheless, I arranged a few
sprigs of foliage to drop down over the
pedestal and thus soften the effect slightly.

Although one has to be careful when
using white containers, as they can distract
the eye from the arrangement, at least
they are neutral and therefore can be very
versatile and useful. I have some beautiful
containers that are lovely to look at but
are very brightly coloured, so although
they can look stunning when used
successfully, they do impose limitations on
the tones and colours of the flowers that
can be used with them. In addition to
white, I think that black and grey
containers are very useful as they tend to
disappear into the background and therefore
don't dominate an arrangement.

When arranging such distinctive flowers as
spider chrysanthemums, give them plenty of
room in the arrangement so they are visible.

The most popular Christmas colours must be red and green, but white, for snow, is a very close runner-up. I know that few of us ever see snow at Christmas, but that doesn't seem to stop us listening to songs about white Christmasses and imagining laden Christmas trees in rooms heated by real log fires! I find white is a very useful colour at Christmas as there are so many different decorations to find a home for that using white as a basic colour helps to co-ordinate everything and give a sense of continuity, making a refreshing change from the cheerful random colouring which can either look lovely or a bit of a confusing jumble.

This Christmas wreath is made from a ring of dry oasis, which can be bought from florists. This is much the simplest method of making a wreath, especially at such a busy time as Christmas, the only drawback being that dry oasis rings are much more delicate and prone to damage than really tough mossed wreaths. For this design, I used artificial greenery, as the leaves do not drop or turn brown and you

Choosing white flowers for Christmas, whether large or small, makes a refreshing change and also provides a good talking point.

can use the finished wreath year after year if you store it carefully in a warm, dry place. Arranging them amongst the greenery, I wired in artificial white berries, dried flowers, pine cones, silver bells and acorns. The result is a pretty little ring that would blend into any colour scheme, thereby making a lovely present to take to a hostess who was giving a Christmas party.

The arrangement shown on the facing page relies entirely for its success on the shape of the stems and flowers. As a bonus, the ginger lilies, *Heychium coronariun*, have the most marvellous perfume. They are ideal for a very architectural arrangement in a large space, such as this hallway, and scent the entire house at the same time. I didn't use any mechanics for this arrangement, but simply placed the ginger lilies in the tall vase after filling it with plenty of water.

Hot Reds

*R*ed is probably the most vibrant and alive colour in the spectrum. It may be the colour commonly associated with danger, but it also signifies warmth and excitement. I find red a very exciting colour for flower arrangements, as it will brighten up a dark corner or give a lift to a room that doesn't get much sunlight. Unfortunately, however, red is not the easiest of colours to mix with others; white might be the one that instantly springs to mind as the best option, but traditionally, red and white is not a popular combination as it seems reminiscent of hospitals, or the Red Cross, and so is meant to be unlucky. Green is supposed to be an unlucky colour too, but heeding that tradition would make the flower arranger's life a little difficult, wouldn't it?

Mixing red with blue or purple can be very tricky as success or failure will depend on the shade of red that has been chosen. An orangey-red does not harmonise well with a royal blue or purple, and a burgundy red can look stunning with pinks and creams but not so good with warmer tones. Experimentation is the only answer, so try the various colours together and discover your own likes and dislikes.

These red poppies shine brightly and cheerfully through the thick grass.

Red is a colour that always seems to come into its own at Christmas, especially when used with its traditional companion, green. Here, I adapted those colours slightly, choosing crimson, bluey-green and cream dried flowers for a lighter, more unusual arrangement.

I'm always looking for new and different places to decorate at Christmas, and had never thought before of decorating my piano. However, whatever the season, I would never use fresh flowers, because no matter how careful one is, there is always the chance of spilling some water and doing irreparable damage to the polished surface, so dried or silk flowers are the only choice. For this arrangement, I mixed some artificial pine with grasses, red glixia and red roses, all of which were dried. To add a festive touch, I arranged some small parcels, artificial fruit and a few pine cones.

The poppies (*see facing page*) have been a very popular arrangement with my friends and colleagues, as most people seem to adore poppies. If one did a poll of the most popular flowers, I'm sure that poppies would be way up at the top. These are silk, because real poppies are very difficult to arrange. Being so fragile and delicate I think they look best left in the fields and hedges, apart from the dramatic huge Oriental poppies that are cultivated.

In this arrangement, I mixed the silk poppies with some artificial cineraria, as the dusky colours go beautifully together and are set off by the black basket. To hold them in position, I glued an oasis 'frog' (available from florists) to the bottom of the basket, then pushed a block of dry oasis on top of it, arranged the foliage first and then added the poppies.

Red flowers look very warm when the weather is cold, making them ideal for arrangements in the autumn or at Christmas.

This is a wreath that could either be a decoration for a Harvest Festival or for Christmas—or any other celebration, come to that! The basic ring is made from dry oasis, and can easily be bought from a florists' shop. The basic structure is made from dried flowers and foliage, including carthamus, achillea and artificial leaves, which I arranged round the ring until all the oasis was hidden. Working on this base, I added dried red rosebuds, pine cones, red helichrysums, green poppy seed heads and lots of little artificial fruits, all of which were wired into place. It is a fairly time-consuming job to make a wreath, but well worth while as it can look really stunning as a decoration.

These roses (*see facing page*) are a good example of how exciting red can be in flower arranging. Here, I have mixed together two very similar varieties of red roses and added some bright red alstroemeria to give a bright, startlingly red arrangement. If you look carefully at the photograph, you will see that the alstroemeria are paler in colour than the roses; this not only emphasises the vivid red of the roses but also makes the arrangement more interesting, giving it increased light and shade.

When an arrangement is as lively as this one, it is important that the container should not detract attention from the flowers, so try to choose something discreet and unobtrusive.

The many moods of red – cooler when used with other colours or vivid and bright by itself.

This dried arrangement (*see below*) is a combination of dark reds with greens and golds, using red glixia, roses and dark red helichrysums, mixed with various grasses, achillea, carthamus and some poppy seed heads. As the container is fairly formal and traditional, I created a classic facing arrangement in dry oasis, making the sides curve around towards the back so that, when viewed from the side, the mechanics would not be immediately visible.

The silk rhododendrons (*see facing page*) are a simple arrangement of single flowers. Using only one type of flower in a vase can look very effective and gives one a chance to appreciate each flower individually – in a massed arrangement, it is the overall colour blend that matters. The flowers were arranged in a block of dry oasis that was taped into the top of the container and then camouflaged with moss, which I held

in place with little 'hairpins' made from florists' stub wires. It is especially important to hide the oasis if you are creating a simple arrangement that does not contain many flowers, as the oasis is then far more likely to be visible than it would be if you were making a massed arrangement, where the sheer volume of leaves and stalks may automatically hide the mechanics. There is no formal way to arrange a simple display of only one type of flower. Instead, you should just place the flowers fairly evenly for a balanced effect—it's very hard to relax near a flower arrangement that is so lop-sided that it looks as though it's about to fall over, no matter how beautiful the flowers might be!

Below: *The deep reds of the dried flowers blend well with the foliage.* Facing page: *The dark shades of the silk rhododendrons make them stand out against the background wall.*

If you are lucky enough to have an attractive fireplace, it can look rather bare during those times of the year when the fire isn't lit. However, there are many exciting ways of filling a fireplace, especially since it will make a natural frame for your flower arrangement. If your fireplace is as large as this one, then dried or silk flowers are a good choice, because replacing fresh flowers once a week could make a sizeable hole in your domestic budget! Nevertheless, for a special occasion it's lovely to be able to create a large, dramatic arrangement of fresh flowers.

When looking for fresh flowers in shades of red and flame, I took care not to choose any colours verging on orange, as I prefer to see the redder shades together. For the foliage, you could choose a variety of colours—a dark copper beech would look marvellous, but my tree has been badly eaten this year so the leaves are virtually all holes!

It is important for the container you choose to fit in with its surroundings, so here I used a copper coal scuttle. It has a good wide base and so will not topple over with the weight of the flowers; an essential consideration for a large arrangement like this.

I filled the coal scuttle with blocks of wet oasis, then rolled up a large length of wire netting and placed it over the top of the oasis, holding it in place with dark oasis tape. First, I arranged the foliage, using beech and some palm leaves to help fill in the centre of the arrangement, followed by a few gladioli. I then arranged the rest of the flowers – lilies, carnations, roses, alstroemeria and gerberas.

The finished arrangement had a wonderfully warm and cosy feel and it stayed fresh for a long time. An extravagance, maybe, but it gave a tremendous amount of pleasure!

When making an arrangement as large, and therefore expensive and time-consuming, as this one, it makes good sense to choose flowers and foliage that last for a long time. You don't want to spend ages collecting up all the fallen petals every day or finding replacements for the gaps in the display if the flowers keep dying. Regularly replenishing the water in the vase will also help to prolong the life of the flowers.

There are so many different ideas and schemes to be devised when using dried flowers, as the scope is endless. Small, delicate arrangements are great fun to create and particularly pleasing when made with dried flowers as, having gone to all that time and trouble to fiddle with the arrangement until one is happy with it, it will then last forever – well, several years, anyway! Here (*see above*), I have filled one of my favourite cups and saucers with some dry oasis, taped in place with a little white oasis tape, then arranged in it a combination of dried pinky red rosebuds, lavender and a few pieces of statice. The lavender is doubly attractive as not only does it look very pretty but it also smells lovely. After all, the scent of a flower arrangement is every bit as important as the colour, since it gives an added dimension to any display.

The wreath on the facing page is another Christmassy blend of blue-green, with sprigs of eucalyptus used to cover the base of a dry oasis ring. The cream poppy seed heads, wheat and barley ears have been dipped in iridescent glitter and give a lovely fantasy feel to the arrangement, making a pleasant change from the gold and silver sprays that are so often used for festive arrangements. The cherries are also artificial but they certainly fooled my dog, who looked extremely crestfallen when I removed a badly damaged plastic cherry from her mouth!

The versatility of dried flowers makes them equally suitable for simple arrangements (above) and more complicated designs, such as a wreath (facing page).

These tulips remind me of a very special hat – or a rather unorthodox hairstyle! This is a very pretty way of displaying tulips that is also very simple, as you are allowing them to follow their natural inclination to bend over, rather than trying to force them to stay upright. For the container, I chose a glass cube and filled it three-quarters full with marbles, then poured in plenty of water. This makes the marbles, or glass nuggets, as they are more correctly termed, shine like crystal, and they can look pretty as a decoration on their own! I then arranged the tulips at random, mixing some lighter pink ones with the red ones to give a colour contrast. Here, I used between fifty and sixty tulips, but if you are only working with a few, this style of arrangement doesn't work as well, since it will look rather meagre when finished.

The red hydrangeas in the kitchen fireplace (*see facing page*) are, in fact, fresh, and they will continue to look good for many months to come because they dry beautifully in a small amount of water. That said, they also seem to dry perfectly well in no water at all. I placed these in dry oasis, as though they had been dried already, and they look just as good now although several weeks have elapsed since the photograph was taken. This only applies to hydrangeas picked in the autumn—summer hydrangeas wouldn't like this treatment at all!

Some arrangements work well with just a few flowers whilst others, such as the two shown here, rely on a profusion of flowers for their effect.

Afternoon tea can be a very special meal, but sadly one which seems to be fast disappearing, thanks to the busy pace of our lives these days. Nowadays I'm lucky if I can manage a quick cup of tea between other priorities, and there's certainly rarely time to set out a pretty tray and sit and enjoy myself!

However, there are occasions when you can relax over tea, especially if you take the trouble to get out the best china, find your nicest tray cloth and napkins and really spoil yourself. Even taking time to lay the tray properly will make all the difference, but the perfect finishing touch has to be a small vase of flowers, whether it's just for yourself, for guests, or even a tray for breakfast in bed (what a luxury!).

Here, I have created a very simple
arrangement using some pelargonium
leaves mixed with fennel flowers and some
red garden roses and placed in a very
simple container, with no mechanics. Such
a simple arrangement as this has a special
charm all of its own, and is very different
from the more formal and complicated
arrangements that one might want to put

*A simple, easily made, arrangement
transforms a tea tray into something special.*

in other places around the house. You
don't have to use only roses for this
arrangement, as many garden flowers
are ideal for this sort of treatment,
especially when placed in an attractive
jug or glass.

Mellow Yellows

*G*olds and yellows are very popular colourings, and there is a wide selection of flowers and foliage with golden tones from which to choose. The range of yellows is just as varied as those in the red chapter, from the dainty pale yellow of primroses to the brighter gold of daffodils and the more concentrated golden tones of chrysanthemums.

There are many golden-hued leaves to grow, and although most of the variegated plants are cream-coloured, tinged with green, there are also many that are a mix of gold and green, which are very useful to the flower arranger and can also look lovely in the garden. One must also remember that other components can be added to flower arrangements, and that fruits and vegetables can make wonderful additions. Golden fruit and vegetables are easily available, such as yellow peppers, golden pears, ornamental gourds, bananas (though I feel that these have rather limited use) and pineapples, to name but a few. Don't rule out any possibilities for inclusion in an arrangement, because until you try it, you won't know if it works or not. Even using a yellow natural sponge in a display might turn out to be a stroke of genius!

A border of yellow meconopsis around a large copper forms the focal point in the Cottage Garden at Sissinghurst, Kent.

Flower arrangements do not always have to be placed in vases or containers – here (*see below*) I have arranged some dried flowers on a straw hat, which would look very attractive either placed on a side table or hung on the wall. As a base, I stuck a length of cream ribbon, arranged in a bow, to the side of the hat, then glued bunches of grasses, some poppy seed heads dyed brown and finally stuck three dried proteas on top, to hide any stalks that might have been visible and also to give the arrangement extra form and interest. You can either use a hot glue gun for this or a contact adhesive.

I think decorating an accessory, such as this hat, can look extremely effective, and it is relatively simple when using dried or silk flowers as they don't need any water. There are myriad ideas, but as an example, you could place a small posy of dried flowers and some ribbons on a book to make a charming decoration for a dressing table or small coffee table.

It would also be a refreshing change from the standard vase or bowl of flowers.

Many flower arrangers enjoy helping with the flowers in their local church or synagogue, and find it especially enjoyable because they are given the chance to make large-scale arrangements that might be too big for their own homes. For this arrangement (*see facing page*), I chose yellow flowers to complement the lovely golden oak of the pulpit, arranging a mixture of yellow spray daisies and chrysanthemums with roses and alstroemeria, and using plenty of yellowy-green foliage to highlight the sunny yellows. I placed the flowers in a basket lined with thick black plastic sheeting and then filled with blocks of wet oasis.

*Opposite ends of the yellow spectrum – butter yellow flowers in a basket (*facing page)* and straw-coloured flowers on a hat (*below).*

Sometimes, flowers are the inspiration for an arrangement, but at other times it's the container or vase that sparks off an idea.

This photograph is another example of how effective it can be to use containers that are interesting and different. You will find a variety of unusual containers in this book, with perhaps the most surprising one being a washing up bowl (*see p 129*), proving that you don't have to use a vase every time you want to arrange some flowers. As this arrangement was planned for my kitchen, I have used such items as a copper saucepan, soup tureen, earthenware dish or pâté dish for a variety of displays. So, don't despair of not having a suitable container until you've studied your kitchen and dining room cupboards, as you could strike gold!

The oval pottery dish here just cried out for an arrangement in tones of golds, oranges and sage greens, so I decided to make a long-lasting display using dried flowers. As it was intended for my kitchen window sill, it was very important to make it fairly dense, as the light would be behind it. If you want to create an airy-looking arrangement, placing just a few stems with the light behind them is very effective but, with a display like this, the density is important as it gives some extra strength to the colours of the flowers.

To make the arrangement, I placed blocks of dry oasis in the bottom of the container, then arranged a layer of achillea heads to disguise any oasis that might be visible in the finished arrangement. I then added more achillea, yellow and gold helichrysums, pale yellow and apricot statice, some dusky pink carnations and bright rusty-orange carthamus, arranging some of the flowers so that they drooped downwards over the top of the container to break any harsh lines around the rim.

One of the bonuses of placing a wide display like this in a window, particularly if you are overlooked, is that it obscures the view beyond and also looks far more attractive than a net curtain or blind! However, you should avoid keeping it in bright sunlight otherwise the colours of the flowers will eventually fade.

The sunny yellows and oranges of this dried flower display look cheerful on even the dreariest of days.

Both of these photographs are of yellow wedding flowers, but each one has different coloured foliage to show what a difference it can make to the colour of the flowers.

For the big bouquet (*see facing page*), I used variegated green and cream foliage, with some touches of cream and sulphur yellow, and yellow freesias, roses, carnations and *Alchemilla mollis*, but for the buttonhole (*see below*) I have used red strawberry leaves instead, to bring out the splashes of red in the edges of the carnation petals.

The bouquet is a simple handspray or shower. To make this I wired together the foliage in small groups and covered the wires with gutta percha tape. Starting with a dainty group of foliage to create the tail of the bouquet I gradually added the rest, making the bouquet wider as I worked. Once I reached the widest point, I then bent the handle (made from the wires of all the flowers and leaves wired in) into a comfortable crook shape. I then bound in the top of the bouquet, keeping the binding wire in the centre of the bouquet, adding height and creating a rounded end. The top of the bouquet should lean back slightly to ensure an even balance. To finish off I bound ribbon around the handle and tied a large bow at the back of the bouquet. For the corsage, I bound the flowers and foliage together with gutta percha tape.

Using different-coloured foliage will alter the warmth and effect of yellow flowers.

This is one of my favourite arrangements in the book, and certainly my favourite one using fresh flowers. When one is able to work in a room setting as attractive as this landing, decorating it with flowers is a pure pleasure, for it is easy to find inspiration from the surrounding colours and the large amount of space available gives one plenty of scope when planning the size of the arrangement. Actually, I got a little carried away here, because the finished arrangement was about 1.2m (4ft) wide and 75cm (30in) high! I chose a rectangular wicker basket for the container, lining it well with thick polythene to keep it waterproof and then filling it with four blocks of wet oasis which I held in place with oasis tape.

The overall colouring is a blend of

yellowy-greens, creams and golds. I arranged the foliage first, which consisted of a selection of evergreen shrubs to give a variety of shapes and textures, with some larger bergenia leaves placed deep in the centre of the arrangement. The molucella and cream stocks were arranged next, placed in the highest and widest points and scattered throughout the basket to give an overall blend rather than a solid grouping. I then used two different sizes of golden yellow roses and filled in any obvious gaps with some double cream freesias, the delicious scent of which floated over the landing and down the stairs!

Often the setting for an arrangement will dictate its style, and this Victorian landing window lends itself perfectly to a large formal arrangement.

These marigolds (*see below*) are another example of how simple garden flowers, casually arranged in an everyday vase, can look stunning, given the right props and setting. This arrangement is ideal for a last-minute tea party in the summer, when you don't have time to make a formal or complicated arrangement, but nevertheless want to put some flowers on the table.

As a complete contrast to the cosy display of golden marigolds, this arrangement of arum lilies and hosta leaves (*see facing page*) shows what a dramatic colour yellow can be. Hosta leaves are invaluable for flower arrangers as they are available in all shapes, sizes and colours, have lovely leaf markings and are also quite easy to grow in the garden. For this arrangement, I chose a mixture of plain green and variegated leaves, all of which catch the light in a fascinating way. The yellow arum lilies are rather special and not perhaps the kind of thing one might

buy every week, but as a special treat they are lovely and long-lasting flowers that lend themselves to some wonderfully dramatic arrangements.

To create this arrangement, which I think should be called 'Trumpet Voluntary', I chose a shallow black container into the bottom of which I fixed a metal pin-holder. Once I had finished arranging the flowers and foliage into this, I very carefully tipped a mixture of black and clear marbles into the container to ensure that the pin-holder was completely obscured, thereby using the marbles in a decorative way rather than as a medium in which to arrange the flowers. As a finishing touch, I placed some pieces of glass, intended to look like drops of water, on to the leaf at the bottom of the arrangement.

*Yellow flowers can be used for any occasion, from the height of sophistication of arum lilies (*facing page*) to the relaxed homeliness of marigolds (*below*).*

As I said in the previous chapter, fireplaces are an ideal frame for a flower arrangement, so here I have tried to use the fireplace like a picture frame, enclosing the enormous hamper of flowers, two malt shovels and a copper jug in a real still life.

The container is an old hamper that I had stored in the attic but thought would be perfect for a big arrangement. If you are using such a large basket, it is a good idea to nearly fill it with layers of old newspapers or magazines, which not only gives it extra strength and solidity but also saves on the amount of oasis you have to use. You can then fill the top with blocks of dry oasis.

The main skill needed for an arrangement like this is that of extreme patience; it will take a long time to complete because there are so many flowers and seed heads involved. Also, you will find when working with dried flowers that they take longer to arrange than fresh flowers because you need so many of them.

I wired the smaller flowers together in clumps to make stronger colour statements, but arranged singly all the flowers with tougher stems. The overall contents ran to about thirty bunches of various dried flowers, but the finished basket looked quite wonderful and very lavish, so it was well worth the time and effort involved!

The flowers that I used included orange morrison, helichrysums, achillea, brown phalaris, poppy seed heads, lagurus and other grasses, *Alchemilla mollis* (which is a very pretty and useful flower whether it is used fresh or dried), solidago, sandfordii, and apricot and yellow statice. This sort of project needs careful planning of the colours and shapes as it is important to get an even blend of textures and shades. If you intend to dry the flowers yourself, you will, of course, have to allow even more time before making the arrangement.

Of course, if you do not have such a large fireplace, or feel daunted at the prospect of making such a massive arrangement, you can scale it down to something more manageable, as long as the setting is in keeping with the size. That said, I must admit that part of the impact of this display is its very size!

One of the most popular yellow spring flowers has to be the daffodil, which looks always so happy and cheerful, and much the nicest when simply arranged with some more daffodils! For the daffodil arrangement here (*see above*), I have used ivy and evergreen honeysuckle for the foliage, arranging the flowers to look as though they've been planted in the basket. The yellow daffodils stand out in relief against their background of dark green foliage, and the trailing stems of ivy and honeysuckle also soften the bottom of the basket.

Whenever one arranges spring flowers, such as daffodils or tulips, it is easiest to use wire netting, marbles or no mechanics at all, and simply place them in a jug or vase. If you really must use oasis, then try to buy the correct type for spring flowers, as the standard green oasis isn't really suitable for such fragile, sappy stems.

Despite their appearance to the contrary, the yellow chrysanthemums (*see facing page*) are silk, thereby providing a display that can last for many months. I deliberately kept this display simple because not only does it enable one to appreciate the beauty of the flowers but also one never tires of it. Had I made a more complex arrangement, I might have become bored with it. To make it, I fitted a small block of dry oasis into the neck of the vase and covered it with moss, then arranged the foliage followed by the flowers to give a casual but pleasing shape.

Above: *Choosing the surroundings carefully can enhance the quality of the flowers, as this lace background shows.* Facing page: *This vase of silk chrysanthemums will brighten up this window for some time to come.*

A summer picnic is usually far too hurried for one to even contemplate taking along some flowers (well, it is in my house, anyway!) but they can add a lovely festive and special atmosphere to an outdoor meal if you can manage to find the time to arrange them.

Obviously a large pedestal of formal lilies, or something similar, would be completely out of keeping with a casual picnic, but a basket of informal flowers, such as these chrysanthemums, can be wonderful.

I have only used one colour and type of flower as I feel this adds to the relaxed feel

of the arrangement, but being such a bright, strong yellow, the chrysanthemums have a very powerful impact. I lined the basket with a sheet of thick plastic, then placed some blocks of wet oasis inside and arranged the flowers in them. Whenever you use wet oasis it is important to keep

If the sun gets too hot, you can move your picnic arrangement into the shade!

it moist, otherwise the flowers will soon droop, but it is essential for an arrangement like this where, with luck, it will be sitting in the hot sun!

PRETTY PINKS

*I*f you conducted a poll amongst flower lovers, asking them what their favourite colour is, I'm sure that pink would be at the top of most people's lists. There are so many different shades of pink that at least one must appeal to everyone, and it's certainly a colour that I never tire of, especially in the softer, more dusky, shades. Pink can also be a very useful, versatile colour, as there are many combinations that it will happily blend with, and although it is difficult to use it successfully with colours like orange or bright red, many other colours work very well with pink.

By popular tradition, pink is more usually associated with girls than boys. After all, when one is giving a present to a little girl, anything pink is always a hit, but boys are not generally known for their love of pink. However, once they become adult gardeners, there are many men who can rave over the particular shade of a pink rose, dianthus or similar flower. Nowadays, pink is also a popular decorating colour for reception rooms as well as bedrooms and bathrooms, so if you are considering giving someone a flowery present, pink is a good colour to choose if you aren't sure of the recipient's decorating schemes.

This mass of azaleas are in full bloom, creating a sea of pinks and yellows.

Pink roses (*see below*) are my idea of a classic dressing table arrangement – soft, dainty and not too overpowering. When planning the flowers for a dressing table, one must remember that it still has to be a practical work area and if the arrangement is too large, there will be no room for anything else! The patio roses arranged here are called 'Gentle Touch' and were mixed with some soft grey foliage. For the mechanics, I placed a small piece of wet oasis in the top of the candlestick and held it in place with white oasis tape. The combination of grey and pink is always a winner, whether it is used in a decorative way or for flower arrangements.

Making a toning pair of arrangements (*see facing page*) is another idea for decorating a dressing table, with a wreath for the wall and a basket with the flowers arranged around the outside, rather than the inside – you can then fill it with pot-pourri, if you wish. It can look very pleasing to have a small group of

A white china candlestick makes a good container for a few pink roses.

arrangements in a corner of a room.

The wreath is based on a dry oasis ring which has been decorated with lots of statice, pink lagurus, helichrysums and bleached grasses sprinkled with a little iridescent glitter, to make an informal and very pretty wall decoration. When arranging the flowers, all you need to do is insert their stems in the oasis, which will hold them firm. The matching ribbons in a raspberry pink added a depth of colour and echoed the pink of the helichrysums.

To make the basket, I used a hot glue gun to stick all the flowers in place. I carefully removed all the stems from the helichrysums and then glued them firmly on to the handle and around the rim of the basket, interspersing them with daisies and pieces of larkspur. As the finishing touch, I curled some thin raspberry pink ribbons by running them taut over the blunt edges of a pair of scissors, then glued them around the rim and handle of the basket at strategic intervals.

A few co-ordinating arrangements are a pretty decoration for a dressing table.

Using large flowers of a single colour can cause problems, as they tend to look like a solid block of blooms, making it virtually impossible to tell where one flower ends and another starts. One way to avoid this is to mix the colours, thereby giving the arrangement clarity.

Here, for example, I avoided that problem by simply arranging some pink summer hydrangeas with white and lighter pink ones to give a good colour variation, placing them in a large wide basket that allows them to be seen in their full beauty.

Before making the arrangement, I lined the basket with polythene (polyethylene), which should be draped inside and fixed to the edges with staples or adhesive tape. I then placed a block of wet oasis in the middle of the basket and taped it to the sides, before arranging the flowers.

When lining the basket, it is important to use plenty of plastic so that the basket

will hold a good amount of water once it has been filled up—hydrangeas, in particular, are very thirsty. Should a hydrangea head droop and look close to death, it is sometimes possible to revive it by completely immersing it upside down in water, and leaving it for a few hours. This is because hydrangeas can also drink through their flower heads.

Whenever you use a basket like this, it is very important to remember that there may be some sharp pieces of wicker protruding from the bottom of the basket, which can easily scratch any polished surface on which it is placed. To avoid this possibility, you should always place a mat or cloth under the basket—the surface will then be protected against both leaks and scratches.

This basket of hydrangeas is simple yet highly effective and attractive.

There is no hard and fast rule that says flower arrangements always have to be kept indoors and not outside – it can be very effective to arrange pots for a courtyard or patio, or even in a corner of the lawn, to enjoy in the summer. Although these geraniums look real (*see below*), in fact they are made from silk, and I have mixed them with some silk ivy leaves to increase the size of the display, then arranged them in a terracotta pot. I placed some other pots around them and made a backdrop of old wooden beams to make the whole composition interesting to look at. One big bonus of using silk flowers like this is that you have no need to worry about the flowers being damaged or bruised by the rain, nor do you have to water them during very hot spells!

Artificial flowers always look their most

Silk geraniums – instant pot plants that need no maintenance at all!

successful if they are mixed with other silk flowers or foliages that they might be seen with if they were all fresh. In other words, it will ruin your carefully contrived effect if you use a mixture of silk flowers and foliage from wildly varying seasons, as they won't look convincing.

The dried arrangement (*see below*) has been placed in a lovely cranberry-coloured glass dish, with a matching small glass bowl placed beside it. In order to enhance the extremely attractive colour of the glass, I decided to use a bright pink theme for the flowers, including dried rosebuds, daisies and larkspur. To create the arrangement, I cut out a small circle of dry oasis and fixed it to the bottom of the dish with a piece of children's modelling plastic (tape would have been visible through the sides of the bowl), before arranging the flowers.

The pink of the rose buds is accentuated by the cranberry-coloured glass dishes.

When looking around my local church for a spot to photograph, we couldn't resist the colours in this beautiful stained glass window near the altar, as it really is quite magnificent. I then set about creating an arrangement that would be complemented, but not diminished, by the radiant colour of the stained glass.

Another consideration to be made when planning the flowers for a church window is the window sill itself, as you will have to ensure that your arrangement is large enough to be visible yet not so big that it can't sit on the sill properly.

Here, I used a narrow copper trough that seemed an ideal shape for the window sill in question. I also find copper very useful because it fits in with many different colour schemes and looks lovely when it catches the light. There is no need to be discouraged if you have the perfect container in mind but know that it is not suitable for use with fresh flowers, either because it is not waterproof or because it will be stained if it comes into contact with water. If it is large enough, you can place a smaller, waterproof, container inside it, arranging the flowers and foliage carefully around the rim so that your secret isn't visible to inquisitive eyes. Alternatively, you can line the container with a sheet of thick plastic and tape it in place. Once again, you can then arrange the flowers to hide any mechanics that might be visible.

For this arrangement, I used a variety of flowers in different shades of pink, including two types of aster and some of the old-fashioned pinks that smell so wonderful. I fitted some blocks of wet oasis into the bottom of the copper trough, taped them in position and then used a little foliage to cover the oasis before adding the flowers.

When using pretty, dainty flowers like these there is no need to add too much foliage. However, if you are arranging flowers with very little of their own foliage and very strong hard stems, it will be necessary to add some extra foliage to soften the overall effect.

When arranging flowers for use in a church or other place of worship, it is especially effective and pleasing to include a few that are strongly scented.

One of the benefits of having a mantelpiece is that you then have a perfect spot for placing flower arrangements. In fact, there are a great many different ideas you can use on a mantelpiece, from holly and ivy at Christmas to roses from the garden in the summer. Obviously, if you have a roaring fire going all the time, fresh flowers will not be happy for long in such a fierce heat, in which case a dried or silk arrangement may be a better choice. During the summer, however, when the fire is not in use, you have an ideal site for all sorts of floral displays. To make the most of the stunning black marble fireplace (*see below*), I created a vivid splash of colour with an arrangement of old-fashioned pinks and bridal gladioli, which are smaller and daintier than their large cousins, while retaining the shape of standard gladioli. The ones I used here have a fascinating darker raspberry pink

marking on their petals and really are extremely beautiful.

Baskets lend themselves so well to flower arranging that they might have been made for the purpose! I particularly enjoy using them for an informal collection of flowers that includes some of my summer favourites (*see facing page*) —honeysuckle, which not only smells lovely but is such an interesting shape and beautiful colour, 'Doris' pinks which are highly scented and have pretty pink markings on their petals, some white daisies just to add a little contrast in colour and brighten the display, with some dogwood and variegated euonymous for the foliage. A summer flower collection like this is guaranteed to bring a smile to everyone's face – flowers are very good at cheering people up!

Pink flowers can look especially delicate and soft, as shown in these two arrangements.

Sweet peas are another of my favourite flowers, but I do find it sad that they are in season for such a short time, as I would love to have sweet peas all year round. If you feel the same way, then you may find that the best solution to your problem is to use silk flowers as I have done here. One only realises that these flowers are artificial on touching them.

I have arranged them in a picnic basket, with no mechanics, to give them an informal look. There are several shades of pink in this arrangement but I never think

it wrong to mix colours of the same flower – if Nature thinks they look good growing together then who am I to argue? A display of sweet peas in the garden looks wonderful, and the more colours you mix together, the brighter and prettier the arrangement will be, so why not forget whether exact shades match for once, and just have a glorious mixture?

What could be better than a basket of sweet peas? Perhaps the answer is a basket of silk sweet peas, as although you forgo their scent, they can stay with you all year round.

P ink and red may not be a combination that immediately springs to mind when one is thinking about successful flower arrangements, but it can work extremely well, as is proved here. The dark red alstroemeria contrast very well with the large pale pink roses, and I

added some Michaelmas daisies for contrast.

It is always important to include several shapes of flowers in an arrangement as it gives a good overall composition. Here, the large, dominant roses mix well with the dainty Michaelmas daisies, while the trumpet-shaped alstroemeria is a flower

with a good amount of foliage, so it always helps to fill out an arrangement.

To make the arrangement, I lined a basket with polythene (polyethylene) sheeting and then placed a block of wet oasis in the basket before arranging the flowers. As well as being a good arrangement for a side table in a pretty room, this pink basket would also make a marvellous present for a hostess or to cheer up someone who's confined to bed.

This pretty basket of alstroemeria, roses and daisies would cheer up any recipient.

Blue
Nocturnes

*M*auves, blues and purples –
this range of the spectrum
is vast, with an enormous
selection of shades and tones, most
of which blend together well and can
mix with other colours too. My
favourite vision of blue (apart from
the Mediterranean sea!) is a mist of
bluebells in a wood. They are a
flower that looks so much prettier
left in the wild or cultivated in big
drifts under trees, and if you try to
pick them they will sadly droop very
quickly, and you'll feel guilty at
depriving someone else of the
pleasure of seeing them. A bluebell
wood was always my image of a
magical place when I was a child,
and that shimmering sea of blue
surely must rate amongst the best
examples of the colour.

   Mauves and purples are very
difficult to describe, because when you
mention that range of colours
everyone has a different idea of what
they mean. For example, what's
mauve to one person will be violet to
another and purple to someone else.
There is usually a fair degree of
blue in the colour mix and so all
these colours seemed to gravitate to
this chapter. They also work very
well when mixed with blues.

*Bluebells growing in a wood make a
wonderful haze of colour.*

It is not always necessary to make a large impressive table decoration for a special occasion, and there may be many times when you are short on space or time, and just want something tiny to create a focal point on the table.

This arrangement (*see below*) is actually three vases put together to form a circle of swans. Each vase consists of three swans joined together to make a curved group. If you find something similar, you can make a small arrangement for the centre, or leave it plain as I have done here. I kept the arrangement very simple, as this added to its charm, and anything much more complicated would just have looked fussy. In each swan I placed an individual delphinium head, choosing a mixture of white, pale blue and dark blue, with some variegated foliage and a little lobelia, but did not use any mechanics to hold them in place. When using small containers such

as these it is very important to keep them regularly topped up with water, as it disappears very quickly otherwise!

There are some corners in a house that just cry out for flower arrangements, and this little niche is one of them (*see facing page*). I chose mauve flowers to blend with the old, greyish-looking, wood, and used a classic grey porcelain vase to give the arrangement extra height. Firstly I taped a wet block of oasis into the shallow bowl of the container, then positioned the bluey-green eucalyptus followed by the mauve delphiniums, aconitum and lavender. Delphiniums can last very well in flower arrangements but they need careful conditioning first and must be given plenty of water to drink.

From large to small displays, flowers in the blue range of the spectrum make a dramatic and effective display.

atching flowers to a particular object in a room can be very successful and effective if the two are placed close together, as they will complement each other beautifully. You can do this with anything, from a tiny vase to a large piece of furniture. There are many examples of this throughout the book, including flowers viewed against a tapestry background (*see pp 30–1*) and, for contrast, vivid anemones against a carved wooden background (*see pp 140–1*).

Here, I have chosen flowers to match this beautiful stencilled fire screen, using a mixture of silk and dried flowers as an experiment. It turned out very well, as each type of flower has its advantages; silk flowers have lots of movement and dried flowers bring lovely muted colours to an arrangement. The dried flowers that I used here include blue and white larkspur, poppy seed heads and grasses, and for the silk flowers I used some blue-pink sweet peas and mauve wisteria, which I arranged to drape down over the front of the container to soften the arrangement and make it hang as it would if it were fresh.

For the container, I chose a classic white ceramic vase, filling it with dry oasis and holding it in place with white oasis tape. The vase is neutral enough to blend into the background and not dominate the arrangement, yet its small pedestal gives the display extra height.

Using a combination of dried and silk flowers doesn't pose any problems with mechanics because the stems of both types of flower can be pushed into oasis and, of course, neither of them need any water. The finished arrangement can be dusted whenever necessary. You can also combine silk and fresh flowers, as the stems of many silk flowers don't come to any harm when placed in water. Before attempting this experiment, however, I would recommend checking the stems of your silk flowers to ensure they are waterproof before merrily plunging them into a vase of water or a block of soaked oasis. The only combination you cannot create, of course, is that of fresh and dried flowers, as the water will turn the dried flowers into a soggy mess – and defeat the whole object of the drying process!

The plumes of dried grasses accentuate the colour and shape of this silk display.

Pale pastel colours are the perfect match for pine furniture as they complement it rather than detract from it. For this simple silk arrangement (*see below*), planned for the top shelf in a recess, I used pale blue irises and tradescantia leaves for their lovely variegated foliage. To make the arrangement I covered a block of dry oasis with moss and then stuck it to the base of a small black wrought iron stand before beginning to place the flowers and foliage.

Huge heads of hydrangeas need a suitably dramatic setting if they are to look at their very best, and this large Victorian fireplace (*see facing page*) is an ideal choice. The hydrangeas I used here are all shades of blue and mauve, and of both mop-head and lace-cap varieties. They were picked from about ten different bushes in all to get the right graduations in shade and texture. The tones blend together well and give an overall blur of cool colour that contrasts marvellously with the black marble of the fireplace.

For the container I chose a large white ceramic flower pot holder, filled with scrunched-up wire netting, as I wanted something as big as possible to match the scale of the arrangement and to hold enough water to allow all the flowers to drink properly. First I chose some very straight-stemmed flowers for the highest point and the side pieces, then placed flowers with curved stems around the edges and through the middle until I was happy with the result.

*Delicate silk irises (*below*) contrast with the huge heads of hydrangeas (*facing page*).*

Both of the arrangements on these pages rely more on textural effect and colour than skill in flower arranging. It is often much better to let the flowers speak for themselves than to arrange them formally into a shape that seems contrived and artificial. The echinops (*see above*) are a fabulous blue colour with a fascinating texture, and I have combined them with some starry creamy-green astrantias which are also texturally very interesting. The blend of colours is particularly restful and allows one to concentrate on the shapes and forms of the flowers. For the container, I chose a blue and white jug to echo the colour scheme of the arrangement.

The blue collection (*see facing page*) is just that – a collection of all the interestingly-shaped blue flowers that I could find in the garden. The eryngium, or sea holly, is always pretty in an arrangement where you want to add plenty of texture, and the aconitum, buddleia and sweet peas all introduce various shapes and tones. To link the vases together, I filled them all with marbles, the marvellous colours of which add tremendously to the display. Groups like this can look very interesting in a room setting and can be a good way to use a collection of containers. If you have nothing suitable you can use some clean jam jars filled with marbles to make a lovely focal point.

Both of these displays prove that flowers do not have to be meticulously arranged in swathes of wire netting and blocks of oasis to look very effective.

Blue is an especially suitable colour to complement old pine furniture, and the vase of cornflowers was an ideal choice for this kitchen setting. The blue of these flowers is so intense that it's difficult to believe that they are real, and only touching them convinces you that they are. If you want a rather more permanent display in your kitchen, you can, of course, use dried cornflowers and grasses instead.

When flowers are as strong in colour as these cornflowers, I think it is very important to let them shine through in an arrangement and not overpower them too much with other, equally strong, colours, as you can soon hide the beauty of the individual flowers.

Here, I mixed the cornflowers with a few ears of barley, which not only suggested summer fields of ripening grain but also echoed the golden tones of the pine kitchen furniture. The generous curves and simple decorations of the vase added to the rustic feeling.

When creating an arrangement like this it is important to place the flowers one at a time in order to obtain the very natural look, and you should try to get an even shape with an overall weight rather than have lop-sided pieces that have been positioned at random and look as though they are falling out of the vase.

Looking round your own garden, in a florists' shop or even through a well illustrated gardening book will show you how many vividly blue flowers there are to choose from. Some, like these cornflowers, have a very rustic and informal appearance, whilst others, such as delphiniums and meconopsis, are much more sophisticated and therefore demand a different treatment in arrangements.

For example, gentians are the most startling and intense blue, and look magnificent when a mass of them are used together in a fairly small arrangement, so that you can look closely at the pretty flower heads. Violets and grape hyacinths are other flowers that look good when treated in this way.

For many people, the kitchen is the heart of their house, where people congregate and good, nourishing, food is eaten. Flower arrangements with an informal feel are the best way to accentuate this atmosphere.

Agapanthus (*see facing page*) are wonderfully shaped flowers that deserve as much interest for their shape as their colour. Here, I have arranged them simply on their own to emphasise their fascinating shapes. For the container I chose a lovely oriental-style ceramic vase in blue and white, to continue the colour scheme. The flowers were simply arranged in the vase and allowed to fall naturally.

As each year passes, dried flowers become more and more beautiful and are available in an increasing number of colours and varieties, making them a very versatile and useful part of any flower arranger's repertoire. However, although we have come a long way, thankfully, from the dried flowers of a few years ago that seemed to be universally brown, there are still not many blue-coloured flowers that dry well, apart from larkspur, delphiniums and lavender (if you count that as blue). Therefore it's very tempting and satisfying to deepen the colours of others, if you are drying them yourself, with a little blue dye.

Here I have used a mixture of naturally blue dried flowers and those that have been gently dyed, including blue larkspur, helichrysum and helipterum, with grey edelweiss mixed with grey foliage and cream statice for contrast.

Choosing flowers to complement their backgrounds will ensure a successful arrangement. Below: *The dried flowers match the colours in the curtains.* Facing page: *The agapanthus is warmed by the wooden panelling.*

This lovely basket is one of my prized possessions, as it has sprigs of lavender woven into it, so a mauvey-pink arrangement was the perfect foil for the container. A mixture of dried flowers, all of which were chosen for their texture and shape, were used. Some of the colours, such as the mauve of the statice, are natural, while others have been deepened with the help of dyes.

It can be very successful to use only a particular type of flower, such as those that

are structurally interesting, as in this arrangement, or mainly open and rounded flowers. When using dried flowers in an arrangement, one frequently finds those that are spiky or grass-like, and the medium therefore lends itself well to the

Many dried flowers are needed to fill a basket like this but the result is worth the effort!

sort of arrangement that contains dozens of flowers packed closely together in a container to give an overall effect.

COMPLEMENTARY COLOURS

*W*hen they grow in the wild, flowers mix naturally, with no colour bars and no clashes. A great riot of colour in cottage gardens in the summer always looks lovely, forming a marvellous tapestry of varying shades and tones. For other people, a beautiful garden contains only a few well-chosen colours or even shades of just one colour.

Equally, flower arrangements can be composed of a particular shade, as you have seen so far in this book, or of a mixture of colours, as shown in this chapter. Just as colours that are very similar to each other can go well together, so contrasting colours can look spectacular in an arrangement, such as purple and yellow, apricot and blue, burnt orange and sage green, red and green or fuchsia pink and lime green. Yellow and white can look very fresh and invigorating, especially in the spring, as can warm colours, such as reds and pinks, with grey foliage.

Experimenting with flowers is always exciting, so try to forget the rules and instead concentrate on creating combinations that give you pleasure. Beauty is in the eye of the beholder, remember, so it's your opinion that counts!

The herbaceous border at Mompesson House, Wiltshire, is a jumble of lovely colours.

Pink and blue may once have been an unusual colour combination but nowadays it is a very popular mix, both for fashion and for interior design, whether the colours are pastels or very bold and clear.

Even so, teaming blue with pink is still slightly less usual in flower arranging, so it is a good choice if you want to make a display with plenty of impact. For this arrangement, I have chosen dried flowers in a mixture of pastel shades that would be suitable for a bedroom—apricot, dusky pink, cream and lavender.

The basket in which they have been placed has pale pink and blue woven into the body to tie in with the flowers, which include nigella, poppy seed heads, larkspur, statice, edelweiss and some grasses. The overall colouring is very soft but the flowers themselves are full of interest, with their different shapes and textures. For the mechanics, I filled the basket with blocks of dry oasis which I held in place with white oasis tape.

These simple dried arrangements make a charming permanent display for a cabinet.

Contrasting colours are the theme of the two small informal arrangements (*see above*), chosen to complement the stencilled cabinet. I arranged each one in a white china container to lighten the colours of the flowers and make them stand out well on the shelves. If I had chosen any darker-coloured containers, they might have merged into the background of the

cabinet and not had the same impact at all. The dried flowers themselves are sprigs of lavender mixed with statice in shades of pinky-apricot and pale cream. I used dry oasis for the square arrangement, but didn't use any mechanics at all for the flowers in the jug.

For the pedestal arrangement (*see
above*) I used the same colour scheme
but intensified it, choosing delphiniums,
gladioli, carnations, pinks and roses in
much deeper shades of lavender and
apricot, with grey-green eucalyptus and
elder leaves for the foliage. As the
arrangement was so large, I had to find a
suitably-sized container, and eventually
used a round grey plastic washing-up bowl,

*This pedestal display is a burst of mauve,
pink, blue, lavender and apricot flowers.*

filled with blocks of wet oasis that I
covered with wire netting and held in place
with white oasis tape. By the time I had
arranged all the flowers and foliage, only
the base of the bowl was visible on the
pedestal but its humble origins were no
longer apparent!

My inspiration for this colour combination came from the stencilled screen standing behind it. Rather than match the flowers themselves, I decided to echo the colour instead, using silk flowers for a permanent display. Alternatively, of course, I could have created an arrangement in fresh flowers that exactly matched those on the screen. Another very effective way to use flowers in a room is to choose some that echo the soft furnishings in a room, such as curtains, loose covers on a sofa or the covering on a bed.

The container was white ceramic, with a pedestal base, chosen to blend into the background and let the flowers stand out well. I taped some dry oasis into the bowl of the container, into which I arranged a mixture of birch leaves, sprays of variegated ivy, wisteria, peonies, roses, pink and white sweet peas and some small peachy-pink lilies.

These silk flowers have been chosen for their colours, in shades of lilac and pink, which exactly match those on the lovely stencilled screen behind them.

Yellow and white is a wonderful colour combination, as it's bright and cheerful and can really liven up a room. Here are two arrangements which both use yellow and white flowers, but in very different ways.

The yellow alstroemeria and white stephanotis in the terracotta jar (*see below*) is a simple arrangement for a casual setting. To emphasise the simplicity of the arrangement, I didn't use any mechanics but filled the container with flowers to hold all the stalks in place. Rather than evenly space the flowers through the arrangement, I arranged them in clumps for extra impact and density of colour and texture. For instance, the starry flowers of the stephanotis would not have been so striking if they had only been placed in ones and twos.

In direct contrast is the formal basket of fresh flowers (*see facing page*), which is ideal for a special occasion. All the flowers are in shades of cream, white and yellow, with very little foliage. Having lined the basket carefully with polythene (polyethylene), I then filled it with rolled-up wire netting as I felt that oasis would not hold enough water, and also that the ordinary sort would not be suitable for the daffodils and irises.

The backbone of the arrangement is the white lilac and yellow mimosa, and I then filled in with yellow daffodils, white and yellow irises, yellow carnations, pale lemon and cream freesias, yellow roses, forsythia and white prunus blossom. Needless to say, not only did the finished arrangement look very invigorating but it also smelt quite wonderful!

I think yellow and white is one of the freshest and crispest colour combinations of all, as these two arrangements show.

Both of these arrangements are chiefly interesting for their shapes and textures rather than their colours although, having said that, the colour blends are interesting as well! They would be particularly apt for the autumn or winter, and you could place the wreath on your front door when celebrating such festivals as harvest-time, Thanksgiving or Christmas.

The bare branch wreath (*see above*) has a basic background of bleached eucalyptus leaves, which were stuck on with a hot glue gun, then I added some bleached grasses and twined artificial blackberries and cherries around the foliage. Finally I added a cream bow to accentuate the leaves, but a bow in the colours of the blackberries would have been an equally successful alternative.

The flowers in the blue and white ceramic umbrella stand (*see facing page*) are ideal for lending structural interest to garden borders, so why not to arrangements indoors as well? Here, the browny-tan *Rheum palmatum* mix well with the white plumes of the eremurus. The umbrella stand made the ideal container as it held plenty of water, thus allowing the arrangement to last really well!

When creating an arrangement, never forget the importance of texture, as it brings an added dimension to any display.

Blue and lemon may not seem to be immediately compatible, but in fact they make a very sharp, zesty combination that works especially well in spring or summer. In this arrangement (*see below*) I lined a basket with thick polythene (polyethylene), filled it with blocks of wet oasis and then arranged blue delphiniums and cornflowers with yellow roses and spray daisies, adding plenty of variegated foliage and alchemilla. The finished effect is one of a mound of colour that blends together while the individual colours remain distinct.

The mixed basket of flowers (*see facing page*) is not really a permanent flower arrangement as the stalks are not in water, but it would be perfectly possible and very effective to recreate an arrangement like this with dried flowers instead. The purpose of combining these flowers is to make a collection of interesting shapes, and also to create a rainbow of pinks and reds, with a little yellow and lemon for extra sharpness. The yellow, orange, pink, red and raspberry celosia, or cockscomb, flowers are almost too fantastic to be real, with their wonderful velvety frilled heads, and the creamy astrantias are lovely starry flowers that are very useful in many sorts of arrangements. There is also some eryngium, or sea holly, that has been dyed pink.

This selection would make a very interesting arrangement, perhaps if placed in marbles in a plain container to accentuate the shapes and textures, rather than as a very formal display.

Both of these arrangements feature somewhat unusual colour combinations which, nevertheless, work very well.

When I look at this photograph, I can't help wondering why we always place so much emphasis on flowers – this arrangement of fruit and foliage works wonderfully, with barely a flower in sight! The foliage includes variegated hosta leaves, barley ears and some herbs, and I used apples, tomatoes, oranges, gooseberries, grapefruits and nectarines for the fruits.

To make this arrangement, first I lined a long, low basket with thick polythene (polyethylene), then taped some blocks of wet oasis in place. The foliage was arranged first to cover the oasis evenly and to fill the basket, then I began to

position the fruit in the same way as I would flowers, with most of the weight in the middle of the basket and smaller pieces towards the edges. To hold each piece of fruit in place I attached it to the oasis with wooden kebab skewers – cocktail sticks are too short for this purpose. If you want to eat the fruit afterwards, you will have to do so fairly rapidly as the hole in the skin tends to accelerate the decaying process and the fruit can go mouldy quite quickly.

A basket of fruits and vegetables like this makes a marvellous display for a Harvest Supper or Thanksgiving celebration.

These anemones look so glorious together that it seems a shame to mix them with any other flowers, so for this arrangement I only added a little of their own foliage.

You might not choose to combine these colours in the normal way—scarlet, purple, blue and pink are not a run-of-the-mill colour scheme (for me, at any rate!)— but Nature knows what she's doing and I think the combination is quite stunning. To emphasise their bright colouring, I have placed them in two pewter containers with a smaller jug close by.

They also seem to shine out of the photograph because of their dark background. It may look like a very large and intricate piece of chocolate but in fact it is a carved wooden dresser! It is also a very good example of the way in which a clever and interestingly textured background can add an extra dimension to even the simplest floral display, so don't be afraid to experiment or even be a little bit different and daring! Once you start to let your imagination really flow, you will be astonished at the results!

Making several small arrangements with the same flowers, rather than one large display, can look very interesting and make a refreshing change from the more conventional ways of arranging flowers. It is an especially good idea if you are using a few bunches of small flowers that would look dwarfed and lost in one large container.

You can also follow this technique if you have a collection of similar containers and want to draw attention to them, as I have done here. Varying the sizes of the containers will add interest, and you can group them together, perhaps with a few other treasured objects or ornaments, to form an attractive still life. You can also use this idea when making a table centrepiece, filling a few small containers with flowers rather than making one large arrangement.

Incidentally, while you are admiring these anemones, I should add that they are not real! In fact, they are silk and very realistic indeed. I have them in my kitchen window at home and they are constantly mistaken for the real thing!

A small collection of vividly coloured flowers, such as these anemones, will really brighten up a dark corner.

I decided to make this arrangement of South African flowers (*see above*) after they arrived from the market packed into a big bunch and I realised what a nice collection they made with their lovely soft colours. They include several varieties of protea and some ericas. When arranging flowers that are native to one particular country, why not find other flowers that also come from that part of the world? For example, a selection of native Australian flowers can look very beautiful, and colour need not be the first criteria as there are some really interesting shapes and species from which you can choose.

This sunny mixture of red, pink, orange, yellow and cream helichrysums (*see*

facing page) are the perfect flowers for this corner of the room as they really brighten it up. In fact, you get double the flowers, thanks to the reflection in the mirror! These flowers are, in fact, fresh, so have been arranged in a container of water placed inside the wooden box. However, they will look very much the same in a few months' time when they have dried out. They can be left to dry in a vase but I prefer to hang them upside down so that they dry evenly, and then arrange them afterwards, when they bring a welcome splash of colour to drab winter days.

Both of these displays show how effective and arresting a kaleidoscope of colours can be in an arrangement.

ACKNOWLEDGEMENTS

The author and publishers would like to
extend their grateful thanks to the following:

David Sturt
South Devon Flowers
Newton Abbot
South Devon
Tel: (0626) 62057
Wholesale suppliers of fresh flowers

The Flowering Dutchman
Unit 3
Hanover West Industrial Estate
161 Acton Lane
London NW10
Tel: (01) 965 3211
Wholesale suppliers of dried flowers

The Conservatory
26 London End
Beaconsfield
Buckinghamshire
Tel: (049 46) 78151
Retail suppliers of silk flowers

Wren Loasby
Brennels Mead
Highweek
Newton Abbot
South Devon
Tel: (0626) 63096
Stencilled screens and walls

Teign Valley Glass
Broadmeadow Industrial Estate
Teignmouth
South Devon
Tel: (062 67) 3534
Marbles, glassware and chippings

Dovedale
Caerphilly Road
Ystrad Mynach
Mid Glamorgan
Tel: (0443) 815520
Fabrics

Hay Fever
Cathedral Close
Exeter
Devon
Tel: (0392) 56578
For their help with the dried
arrangements on pages 28
and 122–3

Pennyfarthing Gallery
Teignmouth Road
Torquay
South Devon
Tel: (0803) 35060
Artists materials

Warner & Sons Ltd
7 Noel Street
London W1
Tel: (01) 439 2411
Fabrics

Laura Ashley Ltd
Braywick House
Braywick Road
Maidenhead
Berkshire
Tel: (0628) 39151
Fabrics

AUTHOR'S NOTE

Many thanks to Diana and John Hatherly for the use of their home, all their help and unlimited supply of props!; Pat and Gary Long for allowing us to take over their beautiful house without a single complaint; Martin and Diane Robinson, from The Old Bakery, Stokeinteignhead, for the use of their window sill and for sustaining the workers; the Vicar of St Andrew's, Stokeinteignhead, for allowing us to take photographs in the church.

My thanks also to Jane Struthers for a fine piece of editing and to Paul Grater for the excellent photography.